AF407537

The illustrations in this book are vivid and bright to spark discussion and encourage imagination.

I created these quilling illustrations using paper recovered from recycle bins in the various classrooms where I teach. I hope it will inspire you to find ways to reduce, reuse, and recycle too. Caring for the created world is a mitzvah we can all share in.

1

DAY ONE

Day and night,
and it was good.

2

**Oceans and sky,
and it was good.**

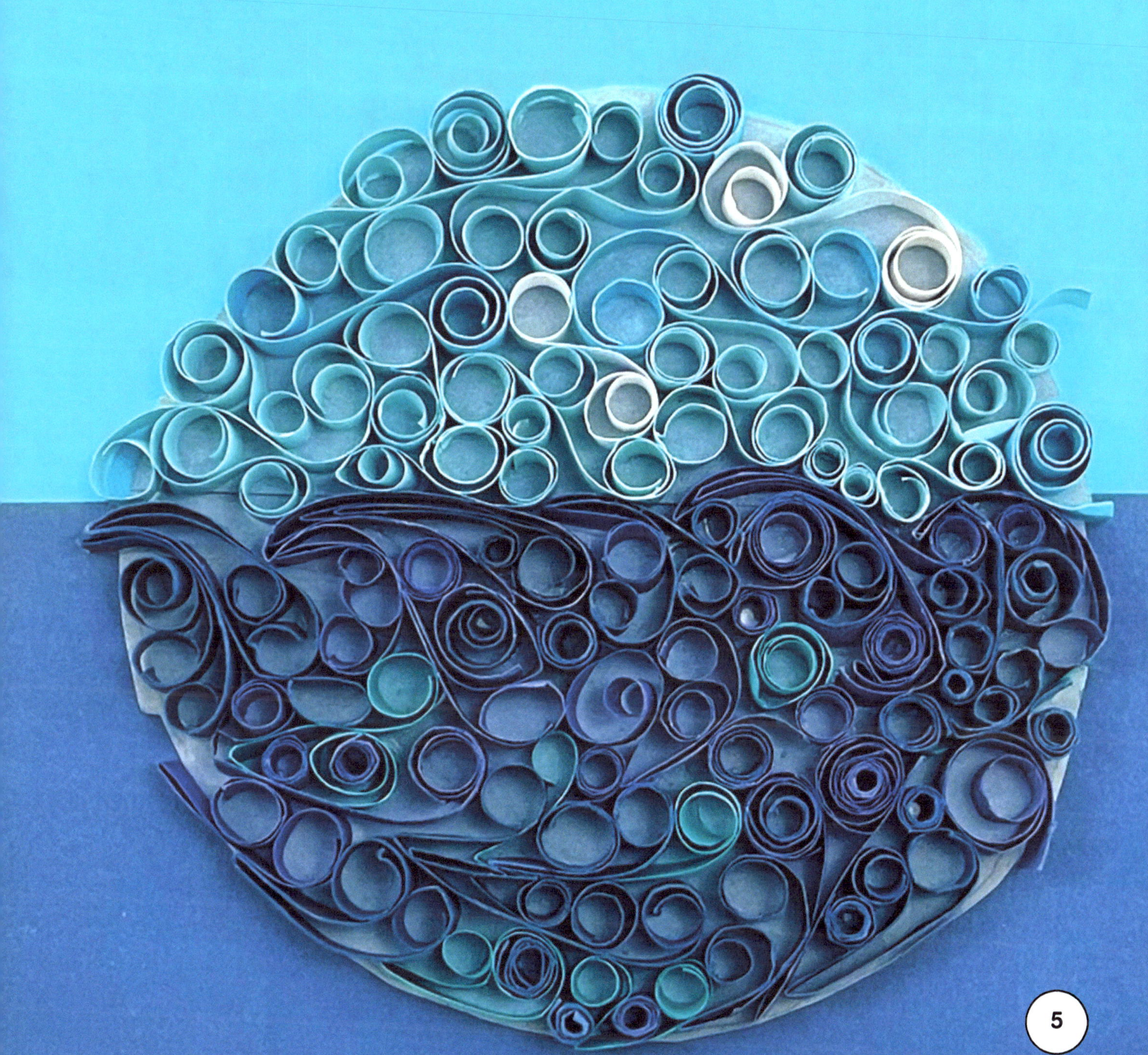

3

DAY THREE

**Mountains and valleys,
and it was good.**

**Plants and trees,
and it was good.**

4

DAY FOUR

The sun by day...

...and the moon and
stars by night.
And it was good.

5

DAY FIVE

Fish and birds.
And it was good.

6

DAY SIX
Animals and humans.
And it was very,
very good.

7

DAY SEVEN

**Day of rest.
Shabbat.**

שבת
שלום

YOU CAN QUILL

1 Don't throw your scrap craft paper into the trash. Keep it for your next quilling project.

2 Use a ruler to mark long strips about ½" wide (12.7mm).

You can make them wider or narrower. It's your art so follow your inspiration.

3 Carefully cut along your lines with a pair of scissors. If you don't have a pair of scissors that is safe for children, ask an adult for help.

4 You now have a lovely straight strip of paper. You can cut strips one at a time as you need them, or you can have fun making lots and lots.

YOU CAN QUILL

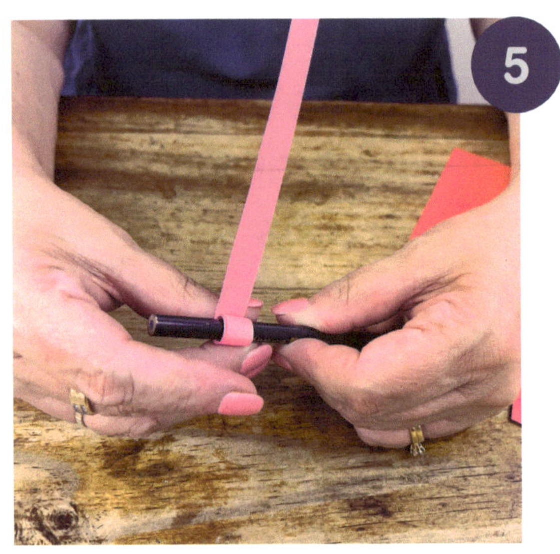

5 One at a time, wrap your strips tightly around a pencil, or something similar.

6 Roll as many as you need to start your project. You may want to create quills in lots of different colors for your picture.

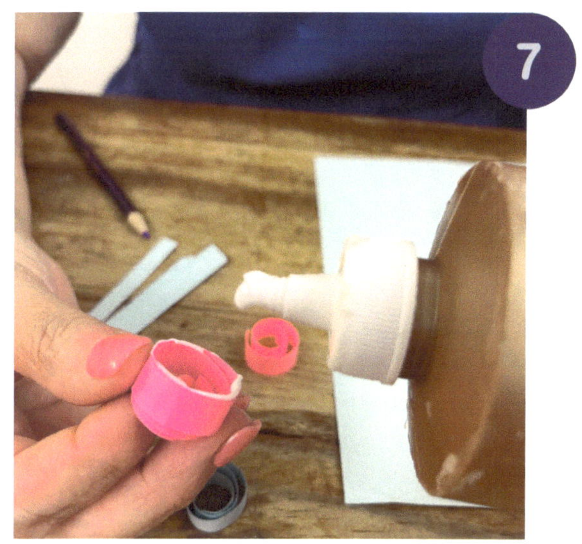

7 Put a nice thick coating of non-toxic paper glue on one edge of each quill. If you like, you can squeeze it on from the tube or bottle, or you can dip the quill in glue.

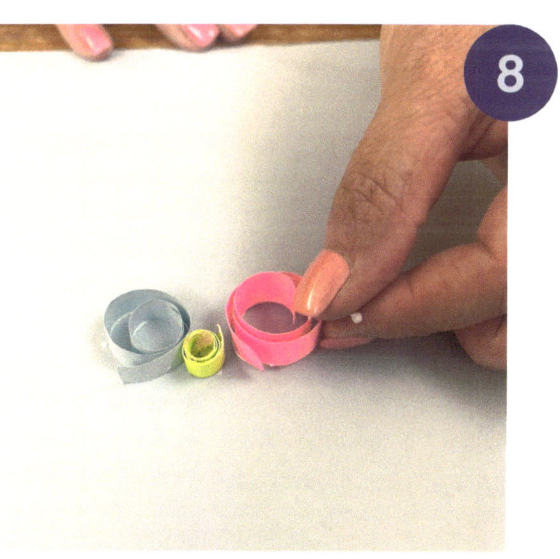

8 When your quill has enough glue, stick it onto a piece of card or paper.

You can make any picture you like, and I can't wait to see your beautiful art!

About Morah Leora

Leora Lazarus is an author, storyteller, ECE educator, and supplemental school teacher.

To the many San Diegans who benefitted from her free Play-To-Learn preschool, she is Teacher Lee. In the global community of Jewish educators she will always be Morah Leora.

Leora has been a groundbreaking developmental preschool and Judaica teacher for over 35 years. Educated at Barkly House Teachers Training College in Cape Town, South Africa, she has gone on to work with thousands of children in Africa and the United States.

Today, Leora is a best-selling author and has a range of teaching tools for Jewish educators, available through her Etsy store.

Visit MorahLeora.com to learn more

You can find all these Morah Leora books, free resources, and more at **MorahLeora.com**

Tree and Bird
A Simchat Torah Adventure
Leora Lazarus

Tree and Bird
A Havdalah Adventure
Leora Lazarus

The TU B'SHVAT Etrog
Morah-Leora
LEORA LAZARUS
PHOTOGRAPHED BY CINDY FRIEDMAN

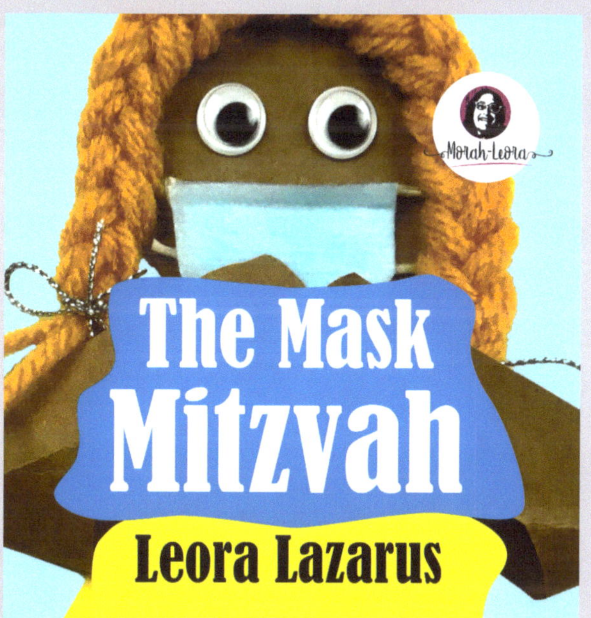
Morah-Leora
The Mask Mitzvah
Leora Lazarus

www.ingramcontent.com/pod-product-compliance
Lightning Source LLC
Chambersburg PA
CBHW042130110726
48006CB00003B/832